GOD'S LOVE CONQUERS ALL

GOD'S LOVE CONQUERS ALL

Keith Ritter

Library of Congress Control Number: 2016912614
ISBN: Hardcover   978-1-5245-3094-5
                 Softcover   978-1-5245-3093-8
                 eBook   978-1-5245-3092-1

Scripture quotations marked KJV are from the Holy Bible, King James Version (Authorized Version). First published in 1611. Quoted from the KJV Classic Reference Bible, Copyright ©1983 by The Zondervan Corporation.

Any people depicted in stock imagery provided by Thinkstock are models, and such images are being used for illustrative purposes only.
Certain stock imagery © Thinkstock.

Print information available on the last page

Rev. date: 09/29/2016

To order additional copies of this book, contact:
Xlibris
1-888-795-4274
www.Xlibris.com
Orders@Xlibris.com
732479

TABLE OF CONTENTS

1st Corinthians 13:1-3

If I speak in the tongues of men and of angles, but have not love, I am a noisy gong or a clanging cymbal. And if I have prophetic powers, and understand all mysteries and all knowledge, and if I have all faith, so as to remove mountains, but have not love, I am nothing. If I give away all I have, and if I deliver up my body to be burned, but have not love, I gain nothing.

CHAPTER 1

The Greatest Love The World Had Ever Known

1st John 4:10

Herein is love, not that we loved God, but that he loved us, and sent his son to be the propitiation for our sins.

God gave up his most prized possession in his son Jesus whom he loved like the world has never known nor seen; and through his death a bridge was made for all humanity. We now have direct access with God through Jesus. His Love, his Forgiveness, his Blessings, and Protection are just a few of the benefits you receive when you come to know his purpose for your life.

1st John 4:7

Beloved, let us love one another, for love is of God, and every one that loveth is born of God and knoweth God.

There is no Greater love than the love of God, God is love and our love comes from God. It is this love that will take many Christians into eternity and grant them everlasting life. The greatest act of love, is dying for someone else in that they might have life.

Jesus was the only one who could die and give up his life for the salvation of mankind that we might live beyond this life as we know it. Jesus paid the ultimate price when he was crucified on Calvary. Jesus is our example of what true love is. He was the sacrificial lamb that was led to the slaughter in which he gives mercy to the unrighteous, hope to the hopeless, and to grace to the sinful nature of mankind.

This was accomplished because of his un faltering, unfailing, unwavering, an unequillble love for us. His dying on the cross was a demonstration and his greatest testimony of proof that he really loves us. Through the Love of Jesus, we received Mercy, Grace, Forgiveness, and Salvation. His love undeservingly bestowed upon us is not based on our obediance or disobediance, or our rights and wrongs, or whether we are a sinner or saint. His love is beyond human reasoning, and in spite of our sinful nature. His love is irretractable. God has a love that is unimaginable because its unconditional. Meaning that there is nothing we can do to earn his love, we can't buy it, we cant sell it, we cant justify it through good works, and we cant achieve it through self righteousness.

The love God gives us is perfect, pure, Holy, and eternal. God gave us his most prized possession to the world in Jesus to show his act of love. Jesus, saw what his Father did and out of obedience and love he wanted to do his fathers will, what ever it meant even if it cost him his life in which it did. As God was the example of what true love is to Jesus.

Jesus is the example of what true love is for mankind. Jesus paid a price for the love he gave us. We are to follow Jesus footsteps in applying his love to our every area of our lives. We are to develop in his love, grow in his love, and manifest his out pouring of love as we are to love others as Christ 1st loved us.

This true love of Jesus can uplift the broken hearted, heal the sick, give light to the blind, unloose the chains of bondage, feed the hungry, protect you from your enemies, comfort you in the mist of your storm, give you guidance in your trials, give you unspeakable peace and joy, prosper you, bless you, provide for all your needs, restore the lost, forgive all your sins, and shine light into darkness.

The benefits of his love are unlimited, unreachable and undeserving. That's the kind of God we serve, who welcomes us with his love with open arms, to come just as we are. There is no sin to great that the love of God cannot forgive. His love is the greatest power, and force on earth. There is nothing that can come up against it.

His love is alive, and his love is always flowing and moving like the wind and the water, you cant always see it, you cant always feel it, but always, rest assure, God loves you more than you know, and his love for you is always there.

CHAPTER 2

The Love of God

1st John 4:15-16

Whosoever shall confess that Jesus is the Son of God, God dwelleth in him, and he in God.

God is love; and he that dwelleth in love dwelleth in God and God in him.

The love of God, can move mountains, calm oceans, and quiet storms. It can shield you from hurt harm or danger, and carry you in the valleys. Once you discover his love, it can change your life.

When God decided to build the world, he formed the earth with all kinds of shapes and sizes and beautiful colors. When something is designed that is beautiful and perfect, it has the elements and components of LOVE. The best art collection you will ever see in your life is the world in which God made.

God's word and love refreshes you every day, His loves gives you courage in the mist of your storm. When you learn to grow and apply his love to your life, you develop courage, confidence, assurance, strength, peace, comfort, guidance, wisdom, discipline, self control, and a sense of purpose for your life.

God's love empowers you to not only love your self but to love others. Many times people are not able to love others primarily because they are not able to love themselves.

This lack of self love comes in all forms, jealously, mean spirited, judgmental, hatefulness, distrustful, false pride, self-righteousness, selfishness, being conceded, arrogance, unwillingness, boastfulness, stinginess, a lack of self-control, indulgence, greediness, rebellion, destructiveness, weakness, laziness, stubbornness, unhealthiness, carelessness, and disobedience in which all these equal up to an (ISI) Inadequate Self Image. Sadly enough many people choose to live unhappy lives without knowing the presences of God's love is what created them.

Many people believe they can make it in this world with out love, in fact you can appear to be successful on the outside, and earn a descent living and reach a financial plateau that most people dream for, but if you are without the joy, peace, and love of God in your life and if you have never experienced the fullness of God's love in your life, you are an empty vessel. Without knowing or experiencing God's love you can never be fulfilled, satisfied, or completely free to love others or your self. There will always seem to be something missing in your life. Material things will never be able to replace God's love. Money can not replace or buy his love, works and performance will never equal up to the love Jesus shed at the cross for us.

It is not that God's love is missing from your life, but its your love for God, that's really missing. God's love for you is so great that he loved you and knew you while you were still in your mother's womb. He loved you before you came into your own and began to know what love was.

God is love, and all love comes from God. He commands us to Love each other.

John 15:12

My command is this: Love each other as I have loved you.

God tells us exactly what love is, and how to recognize what true, real, genuine love is by the fruits of the spirit.

Galatians 5:22

Here's what they are: But the fruit of the spirit is love, joy peace, longsuffering, gentleness, goodness, faith, meekness, temperance and kindness; against there is no law.

What God is saying is that there must be laws in place for those who are not under the love of God, but rather they are under the spirit of the world, where bad things happen time and time again because of the actions and wrong decisions of people who don't have a personal relationship with Jesus.

The consequences of not knowing him will be one of brokenness, loneliness, and emptiness and anxiety from separation. We need God more than he needs us.

But those who live their lives in the fruit of the spirit of God have unspeakable love, joy, peace, happiness, and prosperity in there lives. Love is mentioned first in the fruits of the spirit. It is love that activates the other fruits into action and compliance. With out love, the other fruits would not have harmony to coexist and would be in conflict with one another. God's systems are systems of harmony, order, peace, and balance.

Children of God who live in the spirit don't need laws, and are not under the law, because they are living their lives according to the commandments of God which supersedes all laws.

The worlds laws are not meant for children of God that are true Christians, because Christians who live there lives in obedience and accordance to God's words, commandments and his will, are not murders, drunkards, evildoers, and whoremongers.

They believe in the one true God of Abraham, Isaac, and Jacob. They are not tossed to and fro and carried into strange teachings (Doctrines).

However, Christians were all something before they were born again to the Kingdom of God. Believers are all X something before we accepted Christ into our lives.

Jesus made us whole again through forgiveness of our sins and dying on the cross. He washes you, cleans you up, forgives you, delivers you, and you have now been redeemed by his blood in which your past sins have been erased, forgiven, and forgotten.

Knowing that Jesus loves you is the greatest feeling you can ever have.

John 15: 9-10

As the father has loved me, so I have loved you. Now remain in my love. If you obey my commands you will remain in my love, just as I have obeyed my father's commands and remain in his love.

Praise His Holy Name!!

If you accept his love by confessing and believing in your heart that Jesus was raised from the dead you are a child of God. If you are a child of God, then you are an Over comer.

1st John 4:4

Greater is he that is in you, than he that is in the world. Every one that loveth is born of God and knoweth God.

When you are not able to love our self, or if you have never learned or been trained to love yourself from God's perspective, not only are you dangerous to your self and surroundings, you are also dangerous to others and those around you.

The world's way of love is Me, Myself and I, which will always, ends in misery, loneliness, depression, despair and emptiness.

God tells us about the manifestations of his love through the the fruits of the spirit.

He not only tells us how to love, but he goes one step further if we miss it by giving us an example we can relate to. That example was Jesus Christ, who was the greatest example of love, and the greatest lover of all times.

Jesus love was so pure and committed to the will of God, that it allowed him to do everything he wanted or needed to do as long as it was in the will of his father and we know that it was, as Jesus came to do his fathers will. He was totally obedient to his Father

He was able to walk on water, fast for 40 days, feed 5,000, then 7,000, heal the sick, cast out demons, break every stronghold known to man, feed the poor, overcome any and every obstacle, road block, mountain, prison gate, sickness, disease, closed door, closed window, closed mind, deficiency known to man.

Jesus walked and lived upon the earth in the perfect will and Love of GOD

There is absolutely nothing on this planet that Jesus him self can not handle or over come. And yes his greatest miracle is that he also conquered death.

There is no human love that can ever compare to Divine Love

If you learn how to apply the power of God's love in every area of your life you will have astounding success in your life. You will have power to move mountains; you will have power to accomplish your dreams and goals in life. You will have the power to lead others to Christ. You will have power to conquer any thing and everything that will comes against you, every challenge, every problem, and every situation.

The holy spirit, which is your comforter Jesus sent to us when he departed will be your personal guide and protector to take you through it, over it, around it, or he will eliminate it all together according to God's will and purpose for your life.

You will have power to be a better husband, a better wife, a better sister, a better brother, a better friend, a better person, and yes a better human being and a better you.

The Love of GOD is not comparable to anything in this world.

You will be more effective, more efficient, more focused, more willing, more capable, more able, more ready, more wealthy, more peaceful, more joyful, more interesting, more committed, more teachable, more trainable, more compassionate for others, more responsible, more sensible, more patient, more loyal, more trustworthy, more honorable, more humble, more giving, more prepared, more tolerant, more truthful, more sincere, more bolder, more aggressive, more determined, and more in pursuit of what you want out of life.

The love of God is a powerful Magnet that draws people to him. We have been given the same power to use in love that Jesus died on the cross for. He also used the power of love to perform many miracles. God wants it to also be in you. If this same love is in you, not only will you be able to do some of the things that Jesus did, Jesus foretold of believers and followers of Christ who would perform greater things then of his day. We are the living promise Jesus spoke of 2,000 years ago.

John 14:12

I tell you the truth, any one who has faith in me will do what I have been doing. He will do even greater things than these because I am going to the Father.

CHAPTER 3

The Essence of God's Love

<u>John 15:10</u>

If you keep my commandments, you shall abide in my love; even as I have kept my Fathers commandments and abide in his love.

<u>John 15: 13-14,17</u>

Greater love hath no man than this, that a man lay down his life for his friends

Ye are my friends, if you do what I command you

These things I command you, that you love one another

Love is the core or root that all good things sprout from. It is the foundation in which we accept Jesus Christ as Lord and Savior. This love shapes our personality and moles us into having meaningful relationships with others. It is this love where we have our very being.

The commandments, laws, statutes, principles, and judgements are woven together by the theads and essence of God's love.

God's, love shapes our lives of what we are to become. Love is mentioned more in the bible than money or wealth, yet most people, even Christians concentrate more on money or attaining wealth than love.

Love is the fountain in which all good things flow.

Romans 13:9-10

THOU SHALT LOVE THY NEIGHBOUR AS THYSELF

Love worketh no ill to his neighbor: therefore, love is the fulfillment of the law.

In order to receive love from others, we must first learn how to give love. We have to learn to walk in the love of God by studying his word, hearing his word, and applying his word in our every day lives. Learning God's love is what unlocks the doors to understanding the bigger picture of God, his nature, and his purpose for our lives.

Love is the international world currency needed by human beings in which we can apply the understanding and fulfillment of the commandments. In other words, if we have no love, how can we understand the true meaning of the other commandments? Love has to be the Launch Pad, or our Point of reference, where all things begin and end.

The essence of love is what brings the other commandments together in harmony, order and balance. All the other commandments have the common denominator, element, and characteristic of love. Love is the ignition that is the underlying foundation to all of the other commandments. Love is the glue that connects all the other commandments together because they are all in the same family related to love. Love helps us to execute and perform our duties and responsibilities in truth and righteousness. It is impossible to execute the laws of our society and Government effectively with out love. The holy commandments of God are manifested in the spirit of love. It is like trying to bake a cake with out flour, or drive a car with out tires. Christ centered Love is the foundation of all things.

The essence of love has to be in everything to work effectively and smoothly. Not to say that things can't work properly with out love, because than can, look around you, most of the world is in chaos to some degree or another. If the world is run by love, it would be a different world than it is today. However, thank God for the body of

Christ, that continues to spread the love of Jesus throughout the world, in which there is still time to come to the knowledge and essence of God's love

If you permit and allow the essence of God's love to flow through your life, and be the center of your life, your life will change dramatically for the better. You will have better relationships with those around you. You will have better relationships with your family, friend's neighbors and people you have yet to meet. You will have a better outlook at work with your bosses and co workers.

If you incorporate the essence of God's love into your business you will have much success in not only good seasons, but also in the lean seasons as The Lords hand will be upon your heart to instruct you, lead you and guide your business.

You will reap the benefits of the fruits of love in every area of your life.

Song of Solomon 2:4

We will be glad and rejoice in thee, we will remember thy love more than wine: The upright love thee.

CHAPTER 4

The Spirit of God's Love

Isaiah 44:3

For I will pour water upon him that is thirsty, and floods upon the dry ground: I will pour my spirit upon thy seed, and my blessings upon thy offspring.

God only wants the very best for you and all his creations, He not only wants you to prosper and have good success, he wants your offspring's, relatives, friends, neighbors, people you have never met, and people you will never meet to be prosperous and successful, and happy.

This could not happen if the spirit of God's love was not apart of The Father, The Son, and The Holy Ghost.

I believe the thread that connects all three is Love.

The Spirit of GOD is LOVE.

The spirit of God's love should be seen and recognized in those who know him and have a relationship with him. The spirit of God's love should be seen also in you if you are a born again Christian and you have accepted Jesus Christ as your personal Lord and Savior.

Many times You will not always see or understand the spirit of God's love but you can see the manifestations of the results or workings of the spirit of love through others.

When someone goes out of there way to help you with out wanting something in return, is an example of the spirit of God's love flowing through them.

Another example is when a parent has to discipline a child, for an act of disobedience, or for something that is not done out of love, even though its never pleasant to hurt someone or see someone in tears, it is sometimes necessary as there are consequences for every action. Life has many trials and challenges we experience on our journey, However these lessons are often for our benefit to teach us and to make us grow. You learn and grow through the trials, and pains, and troubles of this life. The Strength in God's love gives us the confidence and blessed assurance that this storm, trial, and challenge will pass. God's love helps us to endure to the end of our days and conquer everything in between that life throws at us.

The Spirit of God's, love requires us to do what is right, just, and fair. That's why he wants Christians to be involved in every occupation of the world. He wants Christians to stand up and fight for injustices. For he knows the worlds eyes are always on Christians.

The Greatest sport in the world for Christians is when we compete to fight and stand up against injustices.

God through his spirit of love is not going to sit by and let you get away with anything and everything. There are times when he will have to chastise you, to show you his disapproval. God teaches us lessons to learn because of his great love for us. If we are slow to learn from our mistakes, the lord may use more drastic measures to get your attention which usually comes through discomfort. Just remember, The Lords ways are not our ways.

The Lord has many ways to get your attention, it will be something very close and personal that will affect you immediately and get your attention. An example of this could be sickness, a near death experience, the impact of someone else's life that is close to you. It will be something so dramatic that it will stop you in your tracks. God is able to do all things and all things are under is control.

He may give you over to a reprobate mind in that your appetite and lust for the world's desires end up landing you in jail or even prison.

God will use whatever means is necessary, and do what ever it takes to get your attention. Many times there's a special calling on a person's life, that he only discovers after what appears to be a setback, tragedy, disappointment, or hardship.

Many Christians have been running, fighting, and resisting the call of God on their lives for many years. When you do this, your life is going to be a struggle because you are not in the perfect will of God for your life. When you begin to let go and let God, you will see the spirit of God begin to move in your life. Once you stop resisting the call of God on your life you will experience more peace and joy as you surrender and submit to his love. God uses people who are weak and have been broken for his glorious works upon the earth.

The in dwelling spirit of God's love is given freely to everyone that seeks a relationship with Jesus Christ in truth, spirit, righteousness, and faith. When you accept Jesus Christ as Lord and Savior, God releases his power through the spirit of Love by the person of the Holy Spirit welcoming you into his Grace powered by his love. You will begin to feel the spirit of his love instantly.

You now belong to the family of God and you are one of his children.

Praise His Holy Name!!

Romans 8:16,17

The spirit itself beareth witness with our spirit that we are the children of God and if children then heirs, heirs of God, and joint heirs with Christ, if so be that we suffer with him, that we may be also glorified together.

If the spirit of God is love and we are his heirs, then that same spirit of love that is in Christ should also be in you.

CHAPTER 5

The Wisdom of Love

Proverbs 1:2

To know wisdom and instruction; to perceive the words of understanding.

The fear of the lord is the beginning of knowledge

The book of proverbs is filled with many principles and wisdom nuggets from Solomon that are God's instructions to not only prosper and bless you, they can also save your life.

A great many of the worlds business leaders have studied the book of Proverbs for its wisdom, knowledge and advice on doing business, building a business, treating people, and avoiding the pitfalls, traps, and snares, so many people with out God fall into.

The book of proverbs also shows us the value of understanding Wisdom.,

Proverbs 8: 33-36

Listen to my instruction and be wise; do not ignore it.

Blessed is the man who listens to me, watching daily at my doors, waiting at my door way.

For whoever finds me finds life and shall obtain favor of the Lord.

But he that sinneth against me wrongth his own soul: all they that hate me love death.

We have been trained to believe that if we want something for our selves we have to go get it. Many have also discovered along the way the greater the prize or rewards, the greater the price we will have to pay to acquire it. An example would be a person wanting to be a doctor, now we all know the rewards of being a doctor, name recognition, notoriety, prestige, a high income, buying power, wealth, and the opportunity to go into private practice are many of the benefits that come with the territory.

To achieve the rewards of being a doctor, you would first have to attend undergraduate school, then graduate school, then a specialized school of your field of specialty, and lastly you would have to have a residency where you receive on the job training.

Not only does this require a number of years of schooling and money, as the cost of a college education now a days is a small fortune, not to mention, the dedication, hard work, focus, discipline, energy and time you will have to invest to achieve this goal. It's a hefty price to pay mentally, physically, and spiritually. The spirit of God's Love in wisdom comes from staying close to God the Father and his son Jesus by hearing the word, reading the word, and meditating in the word. It is an investment in God that requires a sacrifice of your time, and your willingness to serve him by surrendering to his will, and his ways through submission and humility.

God's love does not have any limitations or restrictions, his love is not bound and can not be held captive. The wisdom of God's love is endless for every man women, and child in the earth to tap into when ever it is needed the most.

The wisdom of God's love is here to protect you, guide you, comfort you, and help you to make good decisions over your life. If you continue to live in the sinful nature, the wisdom of God's love will depart from you. The only way that the wisdom of love will leave you, is if you revert back to a sinful nature.

Benefits of the Wisdom of Love:

Love in the spirit of wisdom is able to adapt to any problem or situation.

Love in the spirit of wisdom knows how to handle all problems.

Love in the spirit of wisdom knows how to solved all problems/ conflicts.

Love in the spirit of wisdom knows how to protect you.

Love in the spirit of wisdom knows how to direct your steps.

Love in the spirit of wisdom knows how to provide for your needs.

Love in the spirit of wisdom knows the things you need before you do.

Love in the spirit of wisdom renews itself constantly and will refresh you daily.

Love in the spirit of wisdom sees, down the road, and informs you of what's ahead.

Love in the spirit of wisdom shows you opportunities in all areas of your life.

Love in the spirit of wisdom gives you happiness, joy, peace, comfort, and courage to run your race.

Love in the spirit of wisdom keeps you in line with GOD's Will and plans for your life.

Love in the spirit of wisdom shows you how to manage your finances and build wealth.

Love in the spirit of wisdom helps you and shows you how to make good decisions.

Love in the Spirit of wisdom teaches you how to treat others; how to live and work with others. It also shows you how to have compassion, tolerance, and acceptance of others.

To find the wisdom of God's love, you have to go where the spirit of God's love leads you. You have to go where his house is, his word is, and his spirit is. God's love is perfected in Christians through his presence of love. His love is closer than you think. The Holy Spirit will take you there if you ask.

His house is in the church, his word is in the bible is, and his spirit is in the HOLY SPIRIT, that he freely gives to his children and those that know his voice. Do you know the voice of the Lord? If not, ask him to come into your life and make his presence known to you and he will.

Working in the wisdom of Love will be one of the greatest experiences in life. As you develop a relationship with the wisdom of love, you will begin to listen, hear, understand, and make good decisions. You will see the fullness of things and know whether they will be good for you or bad for you.

You will build up and develop in confidence, strength and courage, as you begin to see things as they really are. The Wisdom of Love opens not only your physical eyes, but more importantly it opens your spiritual eyes. When others try to influence you to walk down the path of unrighteousness the wisdom of love is there to help you resist. When peer pressures are upon you and you struggle with acceptance issues, the wisdom of love will tell you that you are accepted by the Most High GOD, and I will keep you in perfect peace whose eyes are stayed on me.

CHAPTER 6

The Worlds Love

Proverbs 4:23

Guard your heart above all else, for it determines the course of your life.

John 3:16

For God so loved the world that he gave his only begotten son, that who ever believes in him shall not perish but have eternal life.

The worlds love is conditional and subject to change at any given time.

Where as God's Love is Unconditional and never changes.

The worlds love is selfish, and often motivated by a physical tangible objects. It's a love that's based on gratification, self mutilation, with out hesitation, which often leads to devastation. The worlds love is incapable of giving us the kind of love that God gives us.

The worlds love is based on the superficial or often artificial emotions of love. Worldly love is often motivated by greed, pride, narcissism, status, stature, or performance. It's a love that blinds you into doing evil and wicked things out side the realm of God. The worlds love worships man made objects: Houses, Cars, Jewelry, Furniture, Clothes, Money, Boats. The world's love is created by man made hands, and is often associated with an object and comes with a price tag. The riches, wealth, and peace of God's love is manifested through the spirit.

The worlds love has conditions and hidden agendas; people love you for what you can do for them. People love you for different reason. The worlds love is not sustainable. The worlds love is limited in that it only goes to the extent of which another human being is capable of given it. Many people want to love, and they even use words of Love that oftentimes have very little meaning. When a man tells a woman he loves her, a woman should qualify that professed love for her to see if it is actually true love or sleep with me love.

The worlds love grows old, stale, and switches on and off at any given time. The worlds love is unfulfilling, temporary, short term, It is not consistent with the love GOD has for us. The worlds love is filled with emotions and feelings that change like the wind.

God loves you for who you are, what you are, and whose you are.

The worlds love is bias, prejudice, judgmental, subjective, untrustworthy, and pretentious. The worlds love in temporary, God's love is everlasting and will never die. The worlds love is powerless,

God's love can move mountains, heal the sick, calm the storms, produce wealth and fix the broken heart, break down barriers.

The worlds loves are never satisfying

God's, love replenish and refreshes daily

The worlds love is jealous, conceded, ungrateful, impatient, and disloyal

God's love is Pure, Holy, Honest, Forgiving, Kind, Patient, Joyful, Sincere, Caring, Powerful, Wise, Strong, Enduring, Merciful, Undeserving,

The worlds love will always be unpaid

God's Love is paid in full

The worlds loves come with out sacrifice

GOD's Love paid the Ultimate sacrifice with his only begotten son Jesus Christ.

CHAPTER 7

The Love of Christ

John 13:34

A new commandment I give unto you, That you love one another; as I have loved you. Humans are not capable of loving one another as Christ loves us. God's love is a supernatural love based on purity and Holiness. Jesus knew and understood the holiness and pureness of the love of God the Father as he experienced it first hand. GOD's love has a special anointing aura around it at all times, its called Deity, a Halo, a Glow, an Illumination, and yes an Annointing.

John 14:21

He that hath my commandments and keepeth them, he it is that loveth me; and he that loveth me shall be loved of my Father, and I will love him, and will manifest myself to him.

Jesus loved his father, he demonstrated this love by obeying his father, even to the point of what his father commanded him to do. Knowing that he would experience emotional pain, physical pain, and separation pain. He faced ridicule, he was imprisoned, and beaten. No one looks forward to these kinds of things, no one looks forward to dying, and Jesus in his human flesh didn't look forward to dying either, especially in such a brutal way.

But Jesus proved his love for his father was far more greater than his his love for him self by dying on the cross. He said no man taketh my life but I freely give it to show the love I have for my father to do his will. He knew that this act of love would wash away all the sins of humanity, and give everyone a fresh start who so ever called on his name.

Through Jesus Christ suffering he knew that he would rise again as his father God told him so. He knew that end result of him dying on the cross would be much greater than just staying with his disciples. His mission and purpose was accomplished at the cross.

John 14:31

But that the world may know that I love the Father; and as the Father gave me a commandment, even so I do. Arise, let us go hence.

Do you really love the Lord with all your heart mind body and soul. Are you obedient in following his commandments? Obeying God's commandments is your true demonstration and expression of your love for Jesus Christ

1st John 2:3-5

And hereby we do know that we know him, if we keep his commandments.

He that saith, I know him, and keepth not his commandments, is a liar, and the truth is not in him.

But whoso keepeth his word, in him verily is the love of God perfected: hereby know we that we are in him.

Every living thing that God created expresses love in some magical kind of way that may be know only to its species.. When you love something you want to be around it all the time, and as much as you can. I love being around the Lord. Just being around God and in his presence gives me joy, peace, happiness, a sense of well being, security, and yes more love. Love can be expressed or shown, even though we speak different languages, and may not understand one anothers dialect.

Love is still the greatest form of communication. Love is God's special language that connects all barriers of communication in all nationalities, tongues, and tribes of the world. My pets a labadore retriever, and a long hared cat may not be able to speak my language and I can not speak their language, However, through God's love they know that I love them and will care for them.

I will feed them, protect them, and look out after them when they are sick. I believe somewhere in their level of understanding, or animalistic instincts they believe this or feel my love for them.

I, on the other hand, know they love me because they follow me ever where around the house I go and even out side. They even follow me places I don't particular want them to follow me, like the bathroom. I know this is only their way of showing me their appreciation, affection, and love. This love to comes from God.

God's love is not just limited to people, it encompasses every living creature on the face of the planet. Have you noticed that every thing has a partner or help mate? Every living animal has a companion. God designed it this way, he wanted nothing he created to be lonely, isolated, alienated, and with out affection which is an expression of love. My dog and cat are best friends even though they speak different languages I believe they love each other.

What God loves, he blesses, and what God blesses he loves. God only blesses those who have a relationship with him, his son, and his holy spirit. The spirit of life comes from God's great love. Everything in the Kingdom of God is measured in love. Living things come from the love of God, therefore, blessing are God's love for the things he has created.

Genesis, 1:20-22

And God said, let the waters bring forth abundantly the moving creature that hath life, and fowl that may fly above the earth in the open firmament of heaven.

And God blessed them saying, Be fruitful, and multiply

Deuteronomy 7:13

And he will love thee, and bless thee, and multiply thee:

God love us so much, and he wants to save us from 1st from ourselves, second from satan, and lastly from the doom and destruction that is upon the earth.. Through his love, he wants to mimnimize the pain and sorrow we often experience in life. By his love he wants to comfort us and love us even more in our time of need. He wants us to see the traps, and snares, and land mines satan has planted to sabotage Christians. Through his love he wants us to avoid the things that are not good for us, and deliver us from the things that have enslaved, trapped, and keep us in bondage. Knowing and experiencing God's love is the greatest feeling in the world, he wants you to received, and enjoy the very best that he has to offer. He wants to prosper you and bless you through his love.

The spirit of the living God which is his Holy Spirit is sensitive and of divine intelligence. He commands respect, honor, obedience, truthfulness, faith, and honesty. He only has one requirement of all who proclaim to love him and accept him as their one true GOD, and it is this:

Deuteronomy 6:17

Ye shall diligently keep the commandments of the lord your GOD, and his testimonies, and his statutes, which he hath commanded thee.

This is his only requirement, and may be the only thing holding you back, stopping you, and preventing you, from receiving all that GOD and in store for you.

The keys to unlocking more of God's blessings and increase on your life are to: Study and Learn his written word in the bible, and to apply the commandments, principles and instructions he teaches us through his love and faithfulness. Honor the love of God in everything that you do.

2nd Timothy 2: 19

Nevertheless the foundation of God standeth sure, having this seal, The Lord knoweth them that are his. And let every one that nameth the name of Christ depart from Iniquity.

Nobody likes to be made a fool of, and God is not going to let you make a fool of him. He wants to see whether you are really committed, and he will know if you are committed based on your keeping of the commandments. He wants to know that your heart is right with him and with your fellow man.

Leviticus 20:34

But the stranger that dwelleth with you shall be unto you as one born among you, and thou shalt love him as thy self: for you were strangers in the land of Egypt: I am the Lord your GOD.

GOD WANTS US TO LOVE ONE ANOTHER IN THE IMAGE THAT HE LOVES US

God does not want us to be afraid of loving another living being besides our selves

2nd Timothy 1:7

For God hath not given us the spirit of fear; but of power, and love, and a sound mind.

CHAPTER 8

There is No Greater Love

Psalms 91: 14-16

Because he hath set his love upon me, therefore will I deliver him: I will set him on high, because he hath known my name, He shall call upon me, and I will answer him: I will be with him in trouble; I will deliver him. With Long life will I satisfy him and show him my salvation.

God's love is so great, and awesome, its difficult at best to comprehend it. His love is so sure that he backs it up with an guarantee of infinity. He even goes one step further and tells mankind some of the benefits and blessings that come with his love.

Human beings, which are all created by God, do not have the capacity to love themselves they way God loves us. The snake oil salesman on the television ads you see every day and every night are trying to separate us from our money. It has been reported that the average person is pitched 30 thousand times a day subliminally. Advertisers are always trying to sell us love in a bottle through the purchase of their product. They want us to believe our lives will change. They tell us our life will change for the better, and that we will be happier. Learning to Love yourself and others the way God loves you, is truly the greatest love of all. Every things sounds better, taste better, looks better, and feels better when the Love of God is attached to it. The Love of God is a joyful noise.

Finding love in a product is all together a different story. One thing that is certain regardless of how it makes you feel, it is not going to last. Only God's love can make this claim. If God's, love is in your life and you are operating daily in his love, your life will dramatically change. The best part of God's love, is that it is without cost.

We say that we love ourselves, but we do things that bring more harm to us than good in the name of love. God's love does not operate against his word. He gives us his very best when our lives are aligned to his will and love. His love is perfect, pure, unconditional, and always for our good.

Here are some of the distorted ways we love our selves in the physical realm:

We eat to much

We eat things that are not good for us

We drink things that are not good for us

We allow the devil to flood our mind and thoughts of inadequacy and believe it

We do things we have no business doing

We try to hide our true self from ourselves and others

Our love can be bought and is often for sale

Our love often times comes with conditions

We speak words to ours selves that are contrary to love

We do not follow orders,.

We are driven by our own ambitions and self interest, be it good or bad, right or wrong.

We mistreat ourselves, maybe even others.

We do not know how to live, therefore we stay in survival mode and believe this is what loving ourselves is about.

We look for ways to escape out of our reality into someone elses reality.

We think pleasure, and more pleasure is the key to love, this is temporary and fleeting love.

We rebel against any one telling us what to do, even if it is for our own good.

Our love for ourselves is subject to change from day to day

We stay in bad relationships

We watch the wrong programming on television.

We don't respect the laws, of nature, man, of God

We sabotage our selves by aiming low,

We abuse and punish our selves from mistakes from our past.

We tell ourselves the wrong things about ourselves

We think the wrong thoughts and think they are the right thoughts.

We believe what the devil and others say about us, instead of what God says about us.

We watch things we should not watch

We continue to be influence by the love of things in the world, and not the word of love from God

We have not learned to conqueror our fears with the power of love

With out God's love playing an active role in our lives, we are walking in blindness, darkness, and are void of understanding, because we can not see the big picture of what God sees in us and has in store for those that love him and know him.

God has put his word on the line for all mankind to challenge in the universe and the world in which we live,. which he created. He challenges us to put his word to the test. He does not have a disclaimer, or fine print written somewhere that gives him a way out, nor does he need one. He is so sure of his word and his love for us that he gave his only begotten son as proof that his love is the greatest love the world has ever seen or known. He gave himself no way out. If his words are not true he has backed himself into a corner.

No other Person, Politician, President, King or Company in the world today can make such a claim. Many have tried only later to have come up short.

If his love is not true, he runs the risk of having the entire world turn on him, even his precious flock (Christians). In the world we have seen and witnessed so many things that we thought were true, only to find out later they were false. God has put not only his name on the line, but he has put his reputation on the line as being someone who has never lied, and cannot lie. Christians have been persecuted and killed for standing on his love as this continues still today in countries around the world. His Love has to be real, it has to be true, or others would not be willing to pay the ultimate price with theirs lives as many of the apostles did.

The Lord thy God backs up everything, his word, his faithfulness, his love, his compassion, his truth, his righteousness, and his awesome power by his spirit.

His love is the only true love we can really trust.

In over 4,000 years his word is still in tack, and his love has never been breached, There is no judgment, nor counsel nor wisdom that can come up against God's Love.

Isaiah 55:11

So shall my word be that goeth forth out of my mouth: it shall not return unto me void but it shall accomplish that which I please, and it shall prosper in the thing whereto I sent it.

Psalm 91:14-16

Because he hath set his love upon me, therefore will I deliver him: I will set him on high, because he hath known my name, He shall call upon me, and I will answer him: I will be with him in trouble; I will deliver him, and honor him. With long life will I satisfy him and show him my salvation.. God is speaking to those who truly Love him and trust him.

John 15:7

If you abide in me and my words abide in you, you shall ask what you will and it will be given.

Love is the nucleus of the lords sovereign power. He created every living thing in his infinite wisdom, knowledge, and understanding in love. He sealed it up with Mercy and Grace, and gave the last final decree which was the death order of his son Jesus to give salvation and eternal life to all Mankind who believe on him.

The Lords love has a built in protection mechanism in it. It looks out for you, and it has your back. God's love keeps you under control by now allowing your tongue, or emotions, or your actions to run away with you and do or say something that you could later regret. God's Love can also save your life in the heat of battle. God's love is a safe haven you can run to for shelter and comfort. and God many times sends people to you when you seek and are in need of counsel. Man and women of God are often sought after as they can give you Godly advice and they can direct and point you in the right direction. They tell you when you are right and you when you're wrong. They only give you things to build you up and help you grow. They reward you, They do everything they can to meet your needs.

They cry when you cry, and are happy when you are happy. They mourn when you mourn and hurt when you hurt. When they help you or give you a gift, they don't expect anything in return,. They only have your best interest at heart at all times.

This is a love you can trust unconditionally the rest of your life. This Is a JESUS Love

THIS IS GOD'S UNCONDITIONALY LOVE>

This is what the true essence of what God's love is all about.

God's love is greater than every mistake you have made in life, His Love is greater than all the times you have failed, got up and failed again. His Love is the wave that carry us, and lifts us up again and again.

The seeds of his love are what make up his Grace and Mercy. His seeds of love are planted in us.

Everyone runs somewhere for protection, humans and animals alike. If it is not to another human being its something that GOD created out of love. Animals run to the forest, Mammals, go deeper and further out in the ocean. GOD created us to run to HIM. Not only to seek him in times of trouble, but to also come to him at the altar with Praise, Worship, Honor, and Respect and Love.

This will be near impossible in the flesh, we are to learn how to worship and love GOD in the spirit.

Romans 8:1, 8-9.

There is therefore now no condemnation to them which are in Christ Jesus, who walk not after the flesh, but after the spirit. So then they that are in the flesh cannot please GOD. But ye are not in the flesh, but in the spirit, if so be that the spirit of GOD dwell in you. Now if any man have not the spirit of Christ, he is none of his.

God is love and his love is always with us in the earth. His love is timeless, ageless, and has no boundaries. God's love is Omnipresent. (everywhere at the same time). God's love moves through the Holy Spirit.

Unless we learn to love in the spirit and manifest works of love in the spirit as GOD see's love, we will never reach or fulfill are greatest potential as human beings.

CHAPTER 9

Jesus the Ultimate Price

Isaiah 51:11

Therefore the redeemed of the lord shall return, and come up with singing unto Zion; and everlasting joy shall be upon their head: they shall obtain gladness and joy; and sorrow and mourning shall flee away.

What is truly meant by the ultimate price? How much and what does it cost to pay the ultimate price for something ?

The word ultimate means when there is no other choice, when there is nothing left, and nothing else will do. When it cost you every thing that you have. The things of little value and the things of great value.

How does one get to the mental state of ultimate value, when are the stakes raised, and the cost increased?

When you have given every thing that you have and its still not enough, you give your most prized possession as the final act of proof that you are committed to the outcome or end result.

Hosea 13:14

I will ransom them from the power of the grave, I will redeem them from death: O death, I will be thy plagues; O grave, I will be thy destruction: repentance shall be hid from mine eyes.

This is the final act, as you know it, everything is waged when you pay the ultimate price. It is a pouring out to the point of emptyness, or having nothing left and the ending of a process or series. The ultimate is Decisiveness, conclusiveness, the highest of the high, its final the total cost of a project.

Something will happen at end of the process or activity, the final outcome of what is to become.

The extreme level, exceeding that of death.

To give everything that you have to save some one, or everything that you hold most dear requires that you give yourself to provide them sanctuary. Jesus traded his life for the lives of many was the ultimate sacrifice.

It takes an act of love that the world has never experienced to pay the ultimate price for our sins. God paid for us in full through his love and his divine spirit, of giving, compassion, longsuffering, forgivness, sacrifice, patience and pain through Jesus Christ the savior of the world.

Mark 10:45

For even the Son of man came not to be ministered unto, but to minister and give his life a ransom for many.

In our worldly system we would consider this as extreme patriotisms and heroic devotion on a human scale. At the time of Jesus death, the inhabitants living on the earth were unable to comprehend the full measure and impact of his buriel at the cross. Even today, many people are missing the mark of knowing God's great love through willful rebellion. God's love has delivered us, it has set us free. It has opened our spritural eyes. It has allowed us to see and feel the love of Jesus in our hearts, in our thoughts, and in our earthly bodies. His death has had profound repercussions on the earth as man and women all over the world are coming into the knowledge and love and intimate relationship of Jesus Christ as their personal Lord and Savior.

To put it in simple terms, the Ultimate sacrifice: is this: The ability to be willing to do and give up all you have to show you love your one true love. This doesn't mean to give up going after them it means the ability to chase her around the world and let her realize you need her more than anything else. We are the bride of Jesus, and his love for us is more than the human mind can comprehend or imagine. We are God's one true love.

Hebrews 9:15, 28

For this reason Christ is the mediator of a new covenant, that those who are called may receive the promised eternal inheritance now that he has died as a ransom to set them free from the sins committed under the first covenant.

So Christ was sacrificed once to take away the sins of many people; and he will appear a second time, not to bear sin, but to bring salvation to those who are waiting for him.

CHAPTER 10

The Power of Love

Psalm 74:6

Thou didst divide the sea by thy strength: thou brakest the heads of the dragons in the waters.

God's love can move mountains. His love can bring peace, His love can forgive, his love can deliver, his love can restore, his love can do miracles, and the power of his love can part the RED SEA.

There is a time in every one of our lives where we need God to move in a miraculous and supernatural way. Plain and simple. We depend on miracles from God. We need miracles from God in our lives more times than not.

We need a miracle of deliverance and protection every time we screw up. We may not be aware that God is doing miracles through signs and wonders every day through out the world in the name of Jesus as was done over two thousand years ago.

The Father, Son And Holy Spirit is not on some exotic vacation. God never sleeps or slumbers.

Psalm 121:34

He will not let your foot slip, he who watches over you will not slumber. Behold he who keeps Israel, will neither slumber nor sleep. GOD is a GOD of action,. He is a GOD that moves, He is a GOD that is still reining on the thorne. He is still working and performing and saving souls on our behalf.

The spirit of God's love is always uplifting someone in the earth. His love works without ceasing. Many miracles are performed through his love daily. Many times in our own lives we are self absorbed in ourselves or the events of the world to take notice. The human mind has a tendancy to choose what it wants to believe. It it does not see the miracle, it assumes they do not exist. We reason there must be a great big sign of outward appearance or display to believe in miracles, We need to see the whistles and bells and the fireworks with our eyes to believe its really a miracle or a supernatural event.

Miracles and the supernatural does not always have to be the big and miraculous. Many times its something very small and might even seem insignificant. God only has to do something one time, and it resonates all the generations and years of the world until he returns. The miracle, and supernatural events he did through Moses when he freed the slaves from Egypt and the parting of the red sea, sent rippling affects that have a major impact or our lives today.

The supernatural healings, and feedings of Jesus and his resurrection also sent shock waves into the future generation past, present, and beyond. God sent the Power of his Love to the end of the last generation of this world as we know it. The power of God's love will continue to the end of the world and return back to him in his Glory which is in Heaven.

God has set us free from Pharaoh, but we are still acting like slaves, with a slave like mentality. Miracles are performed everyday through the Holy Spirit in our lives but we are not noticing it. When God parted the red sea, Mosses and Arron instructed the people to go through the sea. They were told to keep moving to the other side. There is no question this was a visual supernatural miracle they could see.

They had to also believe and trust God that the walls of the water would hold up and allow them to pass through without collapsing and drowning them. This was a move and a demonstration of the Power of God's love and what his love could do. There are no boundaries or limits to God's love.

Through the Power of the comforters s love, the Holy Spirit, many miracles are being witnessed by the world everyday through the spirit of God's love. In other words, the miracle takes place first on the inside, then it manifest it self on the outside. God knew that man would be very crafty and ingenious in his ideas and inventions, and he likes initiative. He rewards those who take initiative through faith, belief, and determination.

He gladly awaits us at the finish line of every trial, every test, every storm, and every challenge. He knows that when we put in the work it makes us stronger, bolder, confident, assertive, and wiser for the next challenge that come our way.

It was the power of God's love that parted the Red Sea for Mosses and the people to cross over, and God uses his love today to part the Red Sea's in your life, telling you to push forward, continue on the path. When you ask God, for something, expect it to happen. You have to move and step out in the faith and love of the Lords protection to cross over to the other side. God's love has parted your Red Sea in your life. Never look back, never stop believing. The Holy Spirit wants us to keep moving to the other side.

The heavy lifting has already been done. This is the Power of God's Love, He is telling us I will hold back the waters for you as long as it takes in order for you to get to the other side. God wants us to take action and move to cross over to the other side. He wants to take us from bondage, poverty, sickness, unbelief, and every stronghold that besets us to his kingdom love that gives us life in the earth more abundantly.

God wants to take all who believe on him and accept Jesus Christ as the Son Of God to the promise land. Make it a point to believe in the supernatural power and the miracles through signs and wonders that God is able to do because of his love for you. All Christians have been promised a promise land that flows with milk, and honey, and abundance, and success, and prosperity.

Numbers, 14:8

If the Lord delight in us, then he will bring us into this land.; a land which floweth with milk and honey

What prevents many Christian from entering the promise land of abundance and prosperity in their lives is, our reality of not seeing ourselves being created in the image of God's Love. Do you see your self as a grasshopper or a giant slayer as King David did.

Remember: satan will always give you a distorted image and view of your self. He tells you that you are small, weak, dumb, stupid, and unloved and uneducated to amount to anything beyond your circumstances. His will try to cast fear, doubt, and lack of confidence in you.

But you were created in the image of GOD ALL MIGHTY, and ALL POWERFUL. God has given you all power over satan. Always see your self as God see,s you. He has called you a king, a priest, a peculiar people, his flock, the sheep of his pasture, a crown of splender and beauty.

Isaiah 62:3

You shall also be a crown of glory in the hand of the lord and a royal diadem in the hand of your God.

Numbers 13: 33

And there we saw giants the sons of A'nak, which come of the giants: and we were in our own sight as grasshopper, and so we were in their sight

Numbers 21:4

And they journeyed from mount Hor, by the way of the Red Sea, to compass the land of E, dom: and the soul of the people was much discouraged because of the way.

If you were to study a grasshopper through observation, you would discover that when they leap into the air, they have no sense of direction of where they will land. It is impossible for them to go in a straight line. They hop all over the place. Can you imagine how frustrating that is. You have people today, hopping all over the place just like grasshoppers.

Three steps forward, four steps backward. They move from side to side, front to back. They are constantly changing their destination and their journey. Where ever grasshoppers happen to land, this is their place.

It is rolling the dice, like a crap shot. Grasshoppers are double minded and feeble, they do not have the ability or capacity to decide where they want to go. But yet God has a special purpose and place for them in the world. We are created in the image of God and are to see ourselves as God see's us. The Power of God's love will take away all of your fears. We are not quarters as grasshoppers are small in size and stature. We are dollars bills, and we are the giants in the land.

God is holding the Red Sea for you to pass through, What are you waiting for?

CHAPTER 11

Applying God's Love

Roman 8: 37-39

No in all these things we are more than conquerors through him who loved us. For I am sure that neither death nor life, nor angles nor rulers, nor things present nor things to come, nor powers nor height, nor depth, nor anything else in all creation, will be able to separate us from the love of God in Christ Jesus our Lord.

Everything that God is we are, everything that God has, he has given to us. We gain access to it through belief in Jesus Christ. The Lord wants us to learn how to take care of the seeds he has given us to plant in the earth. Your life is a seed. Your gifts and talents are seeds. The money he gives you is a seed. The efforts of your labor in your works is a seed. The very words you speak out of your mouth are seeds of life and death. The word of God's Love through his Holy Spirit will teach you how to develop and grow your seeds in the earth. God's love provides the increase, the overflow, the increase, the harvest, and his watchful eye that protects it.

God wants us to learn, study and develop our skills set in the areas of vocation to be the best that we can be and to give our best to the world. God is an expert in everything he ever created. Everything God created is a masterpiece, true Christians are his greatest pleasure and delight.

We are masterpieces, created from a Master creator.

Wisdom Point: *As Christians, the chosen people of God, we must learn how to act, live, and operate on a higher level than the world*

Can you imagine what its like to live in the glory of God's creation. You only get to this state of Glory when you have achieved and discovered what God has created you for, and you are doing it. I am amazed that many people even Christians do not take the time to ask God what area he wants them to go in for their life's work, I did not, I thought business was my calling and it caused me heartache, pain, and suffering, because I was in the wrong field. God has a special calling for all of us.

We attend colleges, and choose many kinds of vocations and endeavors without ever consulting with God. Jesus died not only for our sins, but he died so that he could leave us something that could go beyond the limitations restrictions, and confinements of his human form of a man. Jesus gave us the Holy Spirit, which has no boundaries, restrictions or limitations. The spirit of God is able to be in every place in the world in believers of Jesus Christ, at the same time when he is called upon through prayer and divine appointment. The body of Christ is able to do and accomplish amazing things when Christians come together in the unity and spirit of God's awesome love. He makes his presence known when two or three gather together in our mist. He sees and hears every one of our petitions.

With this in mind, knowing that God's love is the center of all creation. We are made in his image and we share in his identity with him when we come to the knowledge that everything begins and ends with the grace of his love. The same love God gives to us, we are to give back to him, and through him that same love is to filter to others.

When you apply God's love to your work, your family, and your neighbors, you are planting seeds of love, blessings, and prosperity in another person. You have planted the seed, someone else may be used to water the seed, and God will bring the fruit in that persons life as well as yours. When you bless others, you bless your self.

When you give God's Love out, what you get in return is God's love in. Seeds planted in love will always grow to something good. It also receives favor from the Lord. The more you give out the more favor and blessing from the Lord will you bring in.

God is the greatest Physician, Counselor, Painter, Craftsman, Parent, Teacher, Businessman, Friend, Healer, Combat Expert, Global Financial Expert, Planner, Scientist, Storyteller, Historian, Scholar, Lover, Forgiver of Sins, Comforter, Hightower, and the Prince of Peace the world has ever known.

God is all, in all, and is all knowing. The foundation of the world and laws of the world were establishes by God. The Laws of Nature, Physics, Gravity, and the basic laws that govern our society we live by today were all first establish by his Kingdom.

The ingredients of God's perfect love for you to apply in your life are the fruits of the spirit. God's love is patient, kind, longsuffering, holy, honest, pure, truthful, forgiving genuine, and Powerful. It requires patience, not just work but hard work, whereby you have to study, apply, and endure countless test and trials.

It requires strength to say no to the wrong thing and yes to the right thing. Applying God's love requires you to hold back when you have been wronged by someone, when you have been persecuted, and lied upon, when people in your family are against you, and when others have given up on you.

You have to remember to stay strong in the Word and Promises of God and continue to apply his love.

When you are in the trenches and battles and in the struggles of life The road and the struggle is going to seem never ending and long, hard, and difficult. If you learn how to carry out God's love in every area of your life and in every situation you will discover the Lord's, loving hand thru the Holy Spirit will be upon you to hold you and protect you and carry you and lead you through the storm and out of the storm..

After you have discovered how to apply God's love to others, You must discover and practice how to apply God's love to your own life. What you give and say to others, is returned and becomes manifested in your own life.

The cross is our identifier of who we are in the world. It symbolizes God's holy love to others when we wear it. The Cross, the Holy Bible, and Christians are the greatest physical signs in the world today proving God's holy existence. They tell the world that the love of God lives today, tomorrow, and forever.

Jesus became the word in the flesh on the earth. He is the divine proof of a love that is far beyond the very nature of our sinful world. Jesus came to show us how we are to love and apply God's love in the world. Jesus was our example and teacher on how we are commanded to carry out the love of God.

Jesus demonstrated God's love for all of humanity to see and witness, and bring forth in all the world. He left Christians written instructions in the holy bible to help us overcome the world in every area, situation, and trial that we would encounter in life. He also gave us the power to drive back the powers of darkness through his holy love. Daily reading of the word of God is the basis and a solid foundation for a joyous life. God's love is eternal. It will never end.

God gave humanity a special mark which the human eye can not see. This mark is apparent in all Christians. This is his invisible mark of love that can not be removed. The mark of God's love given to Christians is unchanging, unstopable, unmovable, and unshakeable. What a Mighty God we Serve.

CHAPTER 12

Building your Life around God's Love

1st Peter 1:6

so be truly glad.*There is wonderful joy ahead, even though you have to endure many trials for a little while. These trials will show that your faith is genuine. It is being tested as fire test and purifies gold-through your faith is far more precious than mere gold.

God's love can never fail, and nothing can take it away. Based of Jesus love through the Father, God left his mark on history. God is light, love, and life to all that know him and have a relationship in Jesus Christ.

There is nothing in life sweeter than knowing the love of Jesus. His name reflects and illuminates love. When the Lord thy God's love is pouring out of you and flowing into the lives of others, he rewards you with abundant favor in many areas of your life to enjoy, including your works, finances, and your health.

Said another way

When the love of God flows though your life it adds blessing to the lives of others and it encourages them to do good will to their fellow man. The abundant favor and blessing of God's love will begin to manifest in your life.

If the Love that Jesus showed and gave to humanity is operating in your life at optimal performance you can expect great achievements and rewards for your life.

When God's love is flowing through your life and in all areas of your life, you are clicking on all cylinders, Things just seem easier, there is more joy, peace, happiness, money and blessed assurance through the love of GOD.

When you walk in love, your relationship will be better, you will have greater focus and awareness in your life. You will discover how to remain calm and under control from your enemy

God brings the warmth of his love in a cold and dark world. Christ commands us to love one another as he first loved us. Our love for others through God's love is the true evidence that we are really saved. Love means putting others first and being unselfish. Love is demonstrated by actions showing others we care, and not just by saying it. God's love is showing it. God's love is to be exercised through Christians in the world to support one another and the body of Christ, which is his church. This very action in love requires Christians to give sacrificialy of their money, their time, and their works to meet the needs of others and the church. Investing your time, your works, and your financial resources where God is working, is the greatest soil to invest your seed in the earth.

How we treat others shows the nature and the image of God's Love. For he is our Heavenly Father. True Christian faith results in loving behavior; To walk today as Christ did, we must obey his teachings and follow his example of complete obedience to God through an expression of loving service to all people.

1st John 2:3-6

And we can be sure that we know him if we obey his commandments, If someone claims, I know God, but doesn't obey God's commandments, that person is a liar and is not living in the truth. But those who obey God's word truly show how completely they love him.

That is how we know we are living in him,

To God Be The Glory....How Great is Our God

ABOUT THE AUTHOR

Keith Ritter is an International Motivational Speaker, Author, Coach, and Business Entrepreneu. His life took a dramatic turn from the poor house to the palace when he discovered the secret to financial wealth and empowerment Teaching Kingdom Financial Principles. His teachings are based on the Word of God, and he shares with others how to unlock the doors to Financial Freedom, Purposeful Living, Kingdom Investing, and Abundant Kingdom Living by learning how to apply kingdom principles in the marketplace. His Beyond Greatness Break thru Conferences and Seminars are held around the Country preparing, training, teaching, and inspiring tomorrows Kingdom Leaders.

Other Books written by Keith Ritter
Overcoming Lifes Trials with God
Cast They Net Upon The Lords Promises

Contact Information for Keith Ritter

Speaking Engagements, Book Signings

"http://www.freedombookministries.com"
www.freedombookministries.com
email: "mailto:info@freedombookministries.com"
info@freedombookministries.com

For Info on our next Beyond Greatness Break Thru Conferences

email: "mailto:greatnessbeyond@yahoo.com"
greatnessbeyond@yahoo.com

Join us at Keith Ritter Ministry on Facebook

Printed in the United States
By Bookmasters